Panoramic Journey Through

THE GARDEN ROUTE

Panoramic Journey Through

THE GARDEN ROUTE

First published in 2000 by Struik Publishers (Pty) Ltd
(a member of Struik New Holland Publishing (Pty) Ltd)

24 Nutford Place
London W1H 6DQ
United Kingdom

14 Aquatic Drive
Frenchs Forest
NSW 2086, Australia

80 McKenzie Street
Cape Town 8001
South Africa

218 Lake Road
Northcote, Auckland
New Zealand

10 9 8 7 6 5 4 3 2 1

DESIGNER Tracey Mackenzie
DESIGN MANAGER Janice Evans
EDITOR Lesley Hay-Whitton
MANAGING EDITOR Annlerie van Rooyen
PICTURE RESEARCHER Carmen Watts
FRENCH TRANSLATOR Jean-Paul Houssière
GERMAN TRANSLATOR Friedel Herrmann

ISBN 1 86872 394 1

Reproduction by Hirt & Carter Cape (Pty) Ltd
Printed and bound by Times Offset (M) Sdn Bhd

For further information, contact the Garden Route Tourism Bureau, PO Box 1514
George 6530, tel. (044) 873-6314/55, fax 884-0688, e-mail info@gardenroute.org.za

ENDPAPERS *Groenvlei forms part of the Wilderness Lake District.*
PAGE 1 *One of the unusual castle-style homes at Noetzie.*
PAGES 2 AND 3 *Tranquillity prevails at Langvlei, Wilderness.*
RIGHT *The ideally situated Beacon Island Hotel at Plettenberg Bay.*

INTRODUCTION

The Garden Route, rich in natural beauty, is idyllically placed between the Indian Ocean and the Outeniqua and Tsitsikamma mountains. Stretching along the southern Cape coast for some 300 kilometres from Heidelberg to the Storms River, this verdant region is a visual feast of lagoons, lakes, ocean, mountains and indigenous forests. Further inland lies the semi-arid Little Karoo, especially noted for its ostrich farming industry at Oudtshoorn.

INTRODUCTION

La Garden Route (Route des jardins) est sertie dans une place rêvée, entre l'océan Indien et les chaînes de l'Outeniqua et de Tsitsikamma. S'étirant sur quelque 300km, le long du littoral sud du Cap, entre Heidelberg et la Storms River, cette région verdoyante est un spectacle continuel de lacs, lagons, océan, montagnes et forêts. Se dirigeant vers l'intérieur, on trouvera la région semi-aride du Little Karoo, où la ville d'Oudtshoorn est le centre de l'élevage de l'autruche.

EINFÜHRUNG

Die Garden Route ist reich an Naturschönheiten und ideal plaziert zwischen dem Indischen Ozean und den Outeniqua- und Tsitsikammabergen. Von Heidelberg erstreckt sich das Gebiet über 300km an der Küste der südlichen Kapregion entlang bis zur Mündung des Storms River – ein wahrer Augenschmaus, mit Seen und Bergen, Wäldern und Küstenlandschaften. Im Inland liegt die halb-aride Kleine Karru, bekannt für die Straußenzucht bei Oudtshoorn.

LEFT *Storms River lies within the Tsitsikamma National Park and is known for its cool, indigenous forests, as well as for the dramatic meeting of the river and the sea at its mouth.*
A GAUCHE *La Storms River traverse le Tsitsikamma National Park, renommé pour ses forêts et le spectacle extraordinaire offert par l'embouchure de la rivière, dans sa rencontre avec l'océan.*
LINKS *Storms River liegt im Tsitsikamma Nationalpark und ist bekannt für seine einheimischen Wälder und die beeindruckende Mündung, wo sich Meer und Fluß begegnen.*

PAGES 8 AND 9 *The Overberg, western gateway to the Garden Route, is a rich farming area.*
PAGES 8 ET 9 *L'Overberg, où commence la Garden Route, est une riche région agricole.*
SEITE 8 UND 9 *Overberg, westlicher Auftakt zur Garden Route, ist ein fruchtbares Landwirtschaftsgebiet.*

ABOVE *Bungi-jumpers launch themselves off the 61-metre-high Gourits River bridge. Travellers to the Garden Route pass this way along the N2 highway.*
CI-DESSUS *Le pont de la Gouritz River, sur la nationale N2, vers la Garden Route, offre aux amateurs de saut à l'élastique un plongeon de 61m.*
OBEN *Bungee-Springer stürzen sich von der 61m hohen Brücke des Gourits River. Reisende, die auf der N2 Autobahn zur Garden Route fahren, kommen hier entlang.*

RIGHT *The Breede River offers superb fishing and bird-watching opportunities.*
A DROITE *La Breede River, un endroit de rêve pour les ornithologues et les pêcheurs à la ligne.*
RECHTS *Der Breede Fluß bietet ausgezeichnete Möglichkeiten zum Angeln und für das Beobachten von Vögeln.*

PAGES 12 AND 13 *Swellendam, surrounded by vast areas of farmlands* (LEFT), *is one of the country's oldest towns with historic buildings such as the Drostdy* (ABOVE). *Close by, the Bontebok National Park was especially created to save these antelope* (RIGHT) *from extinction.*

PAGES 12 ET 13 *Swellendam, un important centre agricole, est une des plus anciennes villes du pays* (À GAUCHE). *La ville possède de nombreux édifices historiques, tel que le Drostdy* (CI-DESSUS). *A proximité se trouve le Bontebok National Park, créé spécialement pour la survie de cette espèce* (À DROITE) *en voie d'extinction.*

SEITE 12 UND 13 *Swellendam ist von ausgedehnten Ländereien umgeben* (LINKS) *und ist eines der ältesten Orte im Land, mit historischen Gebäuden, wie dem Amtsgericht* (OBEN). *Der nahegelegene Bontebok Nationalpark wurde eingerichtet, um diese Antilopenart* (RECHTS) *vor dem Aussterben zu bewahren.*

ABOVE *The burnished glow of dusk settles over Still Bay's harbour.*

CI-DESSUS *La lumière douce du crépuscule baigne le petit port de Still Bay.*

OBEN *Die Glut der Abenddämmerung senkt sich über den Hafen von Still Bay.*

THIS PAGE *Still Bay offers many outdoor activities: fishing, boating, swimming, surfing, whale-watching.*
CETTE PAGE *Still Bay attire les amateurs de plein air, qui s'adonnent entre autres, à la pêche, au surfing, la navigation de plaisance et l'observation des baleines.*
DIESE SEITE *Freizeitgestaltung in und auf dem Meer, wie Angeln, Bootfahrten, Baden, Wellenreiten und Wal-beobachtung, machen Still Bay so beliebt.*

PAGES 16 AND 17 *Canola fields near Riversdale.*
PAGES 16 ET 17 *L'or du colza illumine les champs de Riversdale.*
SEITE 16 UND 17 *Rapsfelder bei Riversdale.*

LEFT AND BELOW *Discovered by Bartolomeu Dias over 500 years ago, Mossel Bay is a major port along the south Cape coast with a fascinating maritime history.*

A GAUCHE ET CI-DESSOUS *Mossel Bay, à l'histoire fascinante, fut découvert par Bartolomeu Dias il y a plus de 500 ans; c'est un port important sur la côte méridionale.*

LINKS UND UNTEN *Mossel Bay, vor 500 Jahren von Bartholomäus Dias entdeckt, ist ein wichtiger Hafen am südlichen Kap und birgt Interessantes aus der Geschichte der Seefahrt.*

OPPOSITE *Mossel Bay's Maritime Museum exhibits Dias' statue, a replica of his caravel and a beautiful stained glass window.*
CI-CONTRE *Le Maritime Museum de Mossel Bay expose une statue de Dias, une reproduction de sa caravelle et un beau vitrail.*
GEGENÜBER *Das Maritimmuseum in Mossel Bay hat eine Statue von Dias, eine Nachbildung seiner Karavelle und dieses Buntglasfenster.*

ABOVE *Built in the 1830s by Alexander Munro, the houses at Munrobroek are the oldest in Mossel Bay and now display local crafts.*
CI-DESSUS *Les habitations de Munrobroek, érigées par Alexander Munroe dans les 1830, sont les plus anciennes de Mossel Bay.*
OBEN *Die ältesten Häuser von Mossel Bay, bei Munrobroek, um 1830 von Alexander Munro erbaut, stellen heute Kunsthandwerkliches aus.*

LEFT AND ABOVE *Mossel Bay's temperate climate, safe swimming and sandy beaches are a magnet for sports lovers and holidaymakers alike.*

A GAUCHE ET CI-DESSUS *Vacanciers et sportifs aiment Mossel Bay pour son climat tempéré et la sécurité de ses plages sablonneuses.*

LINKS UND OBEN *Ein mildes Klima, ungefährliches Baden und schöne Sandstrände machen Mossel Bay so anziehend für Sportliebhaber und Erholungssuchende.*

BELOW AND RIGHT *East of Mossel Bay, the tranquil resort of Great Brak River provides a welcome escape from the pressures of city life.*

CI-DESSOUS ET À DROITE *Great Brak River, à l'est de Mossel Bay, est un havre acceuillant pour ceux qui veulent échapper au stress de la vie moderne.*

UNTEN UND RECHTS *Östlich von Mossel Bay bietet der geruhsame Erholungsort, Great Brak, eine willkommene Zuflucht von dem hektischen Alltag in der Stadt.*

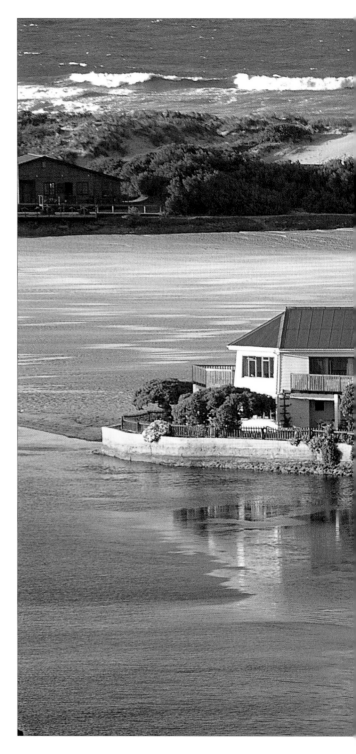

LEFT *The scenic splendour of the Garden Route Dam, just outside George.*

À GAUCHE *La sereine splendeur du Garden Route Dam, près de George.*

LINKS *Das malerische Panorama am Garden Route Stausee bei George.*

THIS PAGE *A rare George lily* (RIGHT) *and George's Dutch Reformed Church* (BELOW).

CETTE PAGE *Un lys unique: le 'George lily'* (À DROITE). *Le temple de la Dutch Reformed Church, à George* (CI-DESSOUS).

DIESE SEITE *Die seltene George-Lilie* (RECHTS) *und die Reformierte Kirche in George* (UNTEN).

ABOVE *Fancourt Hotel and Country Club Estate, a luxurious golfing resort near George.*

CI-DESSUS *Le magnifique terrain de golf à Fancourt Hotel and Country Club Estate, près de George.*

OBEN *Fancourt Hotel and Country Club Estate: dieses luxuriöses Golfanwesen liegt bei George.*

ABOVE   *Only 18 kilometres from George lies Herold's Bay with its lovely beach and good fishing.*
CI-DESSUS   *La jolie plage d'Herold's Bay, à 18km de George, est excellente pour la pêche .*
OBEN   *Herold's Bay, mit herrlichen Stränden und Angelmöglichkeiten, liegt nur 18km von George entfernt.*

PAGES 30 AND 31 *The Outeniqua Pass* (ABOVE), *with its fine displays of fynbos, links the coast to the Little Karoo* (RIGHT), *a semi-arid region with a charm of its own.*
PAGES 30 ET 31 *L'Outeniqua Pass* (CI-DESSUS) *riche en flore indigène, relie la côte à la région semi-aride du Little Karoo* (À DROITE).
PAGES 30 UND 31 *Der Outeniqua-Paß* (OBEN), *der eine besonders schöne Fynbos-Vegetation hat, verbindet die Küste mit der Kleinen Karru* (RECHTS). *Dies ist eine halb-aride Region, die ihren eigenen Reiz hat.*

PAGES 32 AND 33 *The Klein Karoo
is the centre of South Africa's ostrich-
farming industry. De Rust* (LEFT) *lies
near Oudsthoorn, where 'feather
palaces', such as Pinehurst* (ABOVE), *are
reminders of the town's opulent past.*
PAGES 32 ET 33 *Oudtshoorn, la capitale
du Little Karoo, est le centre de l'élevage
de l'autruche. De Rust* (CI-CONTRE) *est
près d'Oudtshoorn. Pinehurst* (CI-DESSUS),
*est un des riches manoirs qui évoquent
le passé opulent de la ville.*
SEITE 32 UND 33 *Die Kleine Karru ist
das Zentrum der südafrikanischen
Straußenzucht. De Rust* (LINKS) *liegt bei
Oudtshoorn* (RECHTS), *wo sogenannte
'Federpaläste', wie Pinehurst* (OBEN),
an die feudale Vergangenheit erinnern.

ABOVE *The breathtaking Swartberg Pass connects the Little and the Great Karoo.*

CI-DESSUS *Le col de Swartberg Pass relie le Little et Great Karoo. Il offre un panorama à couper le souffle.*

OBEN *Der atemberaubende Swartberg-Paß verbindet die Kleine und die Große Karru.*

THIS PAGE *Residents of the Cango Wildlife Ranch include the Cape clawless otter* (ABOVE), *the cheetah* (TOP RIGHT) *and crocodiles* (RIGHT).
CETTE PAGE *La loutre du Cap* (CI-DESSUS), *le guépard* (CI-DESSUS, À DROITE) *et le crocodile* (À DROITE) *sont pensionnaires au Cango Wildlife Ranch.*
DIESE SEITE *Auf der Cango Wildlife Ranch leben putzige Kap Fingerottern* (OBEN), *Geparden* (OBEN RECHTS) *und Krokodile* (RECHTS).

ABOVE *The world-famous Cango Caves near Oudtshoorn.*

CI-DESSUS *Les Cango Caves, connues mondialement.*

OBEN *Die weltberühmten Kango-Höhlen in der Nähe von Oudtshoorn.*

OPPOSITE *The enchanting 61-metre-high Meiringspoort Waterfall.*

CI-CONTRE *La chute d'eau de Meiringpoort plonge de 61 m de hauteur.*

GEGENÜBER *Der zauberhafte, 61m hohe Wasserfall bei Meiringspoort.*

PAGES 38 AND 39 *A little gem along the Garden Route, Victoria Bay is a charming place to holiday* (OPPOSITE), *its sheltered bay a haven for surfers* (RIGHT), *fishermen* (BOTTOM RIGHT), *snorkellers, and sunbathers. During the spring months southern right whales may be seen from the shore* (BELOW).

PAGES 38 ET 39 *Une perle cachée sur la Garden Route. Les eaux protégées de Victoria Bay* (CI-CONTRE) *sont un paradis pour les surfeurs* (À DROITE), *les pêcheurs* (CI-DESSOUS, À DROITE), *les plongeurs et amateurs de bronzage. Au printemps, les baleines viennent dire bonjour* (CI-DESSOUS).

SEITE 38 UND 39 *Ein kleines Juwel an der Garden Route ist Victoria Bay, ein bezaubernder Ferienort* (GEGENÜBER), *dessen geschützte Bucht ein Paradies für Wellenreiter* (OBEN RECHTS), *Angler* (RECHTS), *Taucher und Sonnenanbeter ist. Im Frühjahr kann man vom Küstenufer aus, Wale beobachten.*

RIGHT *A romantic ride can be taken aboard the Outeniqua Choo-Tjoe, a steam train which travels daily between George and Knysna, crossing the Kaaimans River at Wilderness.*
A DROITE *Les touristes adorent l'Outeniqua Choo-Tjoe, le train à vapeur qui fait la navette entre George et Knysna, franchissant la Kaaimans River à Wilderness.*
RECHTS *Eine romantische Fahrt mit einer Dampfeisenbahn bietet der Outeniqua- Tschu-Tschu-Zug, der täglich zwischen George und Knysna fährt und dabei die Brücke über dem Kaaimans-Fluß bei Wilderness überquert.*

PAGES 42 AND 43 *Wilderness: an endless stretch of beach and a peaceful lagoon are among its highlights.*

PAGES 42 ET 43 *Parmi les attractions principales de Wilderness: une plage qui s'étend à l'infini et un lagon paisible.*

SEITE 42 UND 43 *Wilderness: Zu seinen Attraktionen gehört ein endloser Sandstrand und eine verträumte Lagune.*

PAGES 44 AND 45 *Discover the Wilderness by walking through its indigenous forests* (LEFT) *or paragliding* (ABOVE) *from a launching site over this spectacularly scenic area. Other leisure activities include bird-watching, fishing, horse riding and mountain biking.*

PAGES 44 ET 45 *Explorez les forêts indigènes de Wilderness* (À GAUCHE), *ou survolez cette spectaculaire région en parapente* (CI-DESSUS). *D'autres activités récréatives sont l'observation des oiseaux, la pêche, l'équitation et le vélo tout-terrain.*

SEITE 44 UND 45 *Genießen Sie die Umgebung von Wilderness auf Spaziergängen durch die einheimischen Wälder* (LINKS) *oder beim 'Paragliding'* (OBEN) *über dieser wunderschönen Landschaft. Auch Angeln, Reiten, Beobachten von Vögeln und Radeln mit dem Mountain-Bike sind im Freizeitangebot enthalten.*

ABOVE *The Touw River gently meanders through the Wilderness Lakes Resort.*

CI-DESSUS *La Touw River serpente gracieusement dans le Wilderness Lake Resort.*

OBEN *Gemächlich schlängelt sich der Touw-Fluß durch das Seengebiet bei Wilderness.*

ABOVE *Watersports are a popular attraction of the many recreational activities available in the Wilderness National Park.*

CI-DESSUS *Les sports aquatiques sont l'activité principale au Wilderness National Park.*

OBEN *Wassersport ist ein wichtiger Teil der mannigfaltigen Freizeitangebote im Wilderness Nationalpark.*

PAGES 48 AND 49 *Island Lake is one of five lakes making up the Garden Route's Lake District, a region of incomparable beauty.*

PAGES 48 ET 49 *Island Lake est un des cinq lacs formant le 'Lake District' de la Garden Route, une région d'une beauté sans pareille.*

SEITE 48 UND 49 *Island Lake ist eine der fünf Seen, die das Seengebiet der Garden Route ausmachen, eine Region von traumhafter Schönheit.*

OPPOSITE *Groenvlei* (TOP), *a freshwater lake, is a haven for birds such as the brownhooded kingfisher* (BOTTOM LEFT) *and darter* (BOTTOM RIGHT).
CI-CONTRE *Groenvlei est un paradis pour les oiseaux, tels que le martin-pêcheur* (CI-DESSOUS, À GAUCHE) *et l'oiseau serpent* (CI-DESSOUS, À DROITE).
GEGENÜBER *Groenvlei ist ein Paradies für Vögel, wie den Braunkopf-liest* (UNTEN LINKS) *und den Schlangenhalsvogel* (UNTEN RECHTS).

ABOVE *Adjoining the Wilderness National Park is the Goukamma Nature Reserve where Groenvlei is situated.*
CI-DESSUS *Goukamma Nature Reserve, où se situe Groenvlei, est adjacent au Wilderness National Park.*
OBEN *Groenvlei liegt im Goukamma Naturschutzgebiet, das an den Wilderness Nationalpark grenzt.*

PAGES 52 AND 53 *Of the District's lakes, Swartvlei is the largest and, like the other areas in the Wilderness National Park, is a harmonious blend of conservation, recreation and unobtrusive accommodation.*

PAGES 52 ET 53 *De tous les lacs du district, Swartvlei est le plus étendu; comme partout dans le Wilderness National Park, il forme une combinaison harmonieuse entre conservation et centre de loisirs.*

SEITE 52 UND 53 *Beim Swartvlei, dem größten See der Seenplatte, herrscht, wie im ganzen Wilderness Nationalpark, ein harmonisches Nebeneinander von Naturschutz, Erholungsmöglichkeiten und unauffälligen Unterkünften.*

ABOVE *Sedgefield, where Swartvlei enters the sea, nestles between vegetated hills and unspoilt beaches.*

CI-DESSUS *Sedgefield, où le Swartvlei s'ouvre sur la mer, est niché entre des collines verdoyantes et des plages immaculées.*

OBEN *Sedgefield, wo der Swartvlei ins Meer mündet, erstreckt sich zwischen bewachsenen Hügeln und naturbelassenen Stränden.*

RIGHT *Picturesque Goukamma River Valley, a tranquil hamlet en route to Knysna.*

A DROITE *Un hameau paisible sur la route de Knysna... Goukamma River Valley.*

RECHTS *Im malerischen Flußtal des Goukamma liegt ein verträumtes Dörfchen.*

PAGES 56 AND 57 *Knysna Heads, two sandstone sentinels guarding the mouth of the Knysna Lagoon.*

PAGES 56 ET 57 *Comme deux sentinelles de grès, les Knysna Heads gardent l'embouchure du lagon.*

SEITE 56 UND 57 *Knysna Heads, zwei Posten aus Sandstein, bewachen die Mündung der Lagune.*

PAGES 58 AND 59 *Knysna, 'the Jewel of the Garden Route', is a vibrant, colourful town with many varied arts and crafts shops. It has a fascinating history of woodcutters, timber merchants, gold diggers and sea-farers.*

PAGES 58 ET 59 *Knysna, le joyau de la Garden Route, est une ville animée et pittoresque. On y trouve de nombreuses galeries d'art et des produits artisanaux. Son histoire, où participent des bûcherons, des négociants en bois, des chercheurs d'or et des marins, est captivante.*

SEITE 58 UND 59 *Knysna, bekannt als das Juwel der Garden Route, ist ein pulsierender, farbenfreudiger Ort mit vielen verschiedenen Läden und Kunsthandlungen. Die faszinierende Geschichte des Ortes berichtet von Holzhändlern und Schnitzern, Goldgräbern und Seefahrern.*

PAGES 60 AND 61 *The Knysna Lagoon flows to the sea between the Knysna Heads* (OPPOSITE), *and superb views can be enjoyed from a perfectly situated restaurant* (ABOVE) *at the Heads. Scenic trips can also be enjoyed on the John Benn* (RIGHT), *a double-decker cruise boat on the Lagoon.*
PAGES 60 ET 61 *Le lagon s'ouvre sur la mer entre les Knysna Heads* (CI-CONTRE), *offrant un splendide panorama qui peut être admiré du restaurant* (CI-DESSUS) *qui y est situé. Le John Benn* (À DROITE) *emmène les touristes en croisière sur le lagon.*
SEITE 60 UND 61 *Die Lagune bei Knysna mündet ins Meer bei den Knysna Heads* (GEGENÜBER). *Von dem ideal plazierten Restaurant hat man einen herrlichen Ausblick* (OBEN). *Auf der doppelstöckigen John Benn* (RECHTS) *kann man Kreuzfahrten auf der Lagune unternehmen.*

ABOVE *The Outeniqua Choo-Tjoe chugs its way over the placid Knysna Lagoon.*

CI-DESSUS *L'Outeniqua Choo-Tjoe franchit en haletant les eaux paisibles du Knysna Lagoon.*

OBEN *Der Outeniqua-Tschu-Tschu-Zug dampft über die spiegelglatte Lagune bei Knysna.*

ABOVE *The Head to Head Marathon, one of several annual sporting events taking place in Knysna.*

CI-DESSUS *Le 'Head to Head Marathon', une des nombreuses épreuves sportives qui ont lieu à Knysna.*

OBEN *Der 'Head to Head' Marathonlauf ist eines der zahlreichen jährlichen Sportveranstaltungen in Knysna.*

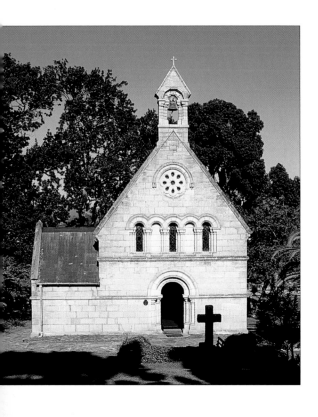

LEFT *Tiny Belvidere Church was built in 1850 from local stone and timber.*

A GAUCHE *La minuscule église de Belvidere en pierre et bois du pays, fut construite en 1850.*

LINKS *Die winzige Kirche in Belvidere wurde 1850 errichtet, wobei man Holz und Steine aus der Umgebung verwandte.*

BELOW AND OPPOSITE *Knysna Lagoon provides visitors with excellent fishing, sailing, boating and water-skiing opportunities.*

CI-DESSOUS ET CI-CONTRE *Le Knysna Lagoon offre aux visiteurs d'excellentes possibilités de pêche, de yachting et de ski nautique.*

UNTEN UND GEGENÜBER *Die Knysna Lagune bietet vorzügliche Möglichkeiten zum Angeln, Segeln, Wasserskilaufen und für Bootfahrten.*

ABOVE *Knysna Lagoon is the hub of a successful oyster-farming and boat-building industry.*

CI-DESSUS *Le Knysna Lagoon est un centre prospère d'ostréiculture et de construction navale.*

OBEN *Die Knysna Lagune ist ein Zentrum für Bootsbau und hat eine florierende Austernzucht.*

ABOVE AND RIGHT *Seafood restaurants, specialty shops,*
pubs and sailing trips, all at the Waterfront, Knysna Quays.
CI-DESSUS ET À DROITE *Le Waterfront offre un choix de*
restaurants spécialisés en fruits de mer, magasins spécialisés,
pubs et d'excursions en yacht.
OBEN UND RECHTS *Fischlokale, ausgefallene Läden,*
Kneipen und Segel-Kreuzfahrten – dies alles und mehr
bietet die Hafenanlage, Knysna Quays.

PAGES 68 AND 69 *Within Knysna's dense indigenous forests* (LEFT) *lie many giant iron-wood and yellowwood trees, such as the Big Tree* (OPPOSITE) *which stands 46 metres high.*

PAGES 68 ET 69 *La végétation dense des forêts de Knysna* (À GAUCHE) *recèle de nombreux arbres géants, tel que ce 'Big Tree' de 46m* (CI-CONTRE).

SEITE 68 UND 69 *In den dichten, einheimischen Wäldern bei Knysna* (LINKS) *stehen viele, riesige Eisenholz- und Gelbholzbäume, wie etwa der 'Große Baum'* (GEGENÜBER), *der 46m hoch ist.*

Pages 70 and 71 *Knysna forest supports the Knysna loerie* (OPPOSITE TOP LEFT), *and an undergrowth of fungi* (OPPOSITE TOP RIGHT), *mosses and ferns. Millwood House* (OPPOSITE BOTTOM), *an old mining house, and Jubilee Creek* (ABOVE) *are memories of the gold rush of the 1880s.*
Pages 70 et 71 *Les forêts de Knysna sont tapissées de champignons, mousses et fougères* (CI-CONTRE, EN HAUT, À DROITE). *Dans les arbres perche l'effronté Knysna loerie* (CI-CONTRE, EN HAUT, À GAUCHE).

Millwood House (CI-CONTRE, EN BAS), *une ancienne maison de mineur, et Jubilee Creek* (CI-DESSUS) *évoquent la ruée vers l'or des 1880.*
Seite 70 und 71 *Der scheue Helmturako* (GEGENÜBER OBEN LINKS) *lebt in den Wäldern bei Knysna, und im dichten Unterwuchs gedeihen Pilze* (GEGENÜBER OBEN RECHTS), *Moos und Farne. Millwood House* (GEGENÜBER UNTEN), *ein altes Bergbauhaus, und Jubilee Creek* (OBEN) *erinnern an den Goldrausch um 1880.*

RIGHT *Eleven kilometres west of Knysna lies Noetzie where stone 'castles' have been built as private holiday homes.*

A DROITE *Noetzie, à 11km à l'ouest de Knysna, où les résidences secondaires sont des 'chateaux'.*

RECHTS *Elf Kilometer westlich von Knysna liegt Noetzie, wo einige Ferienhäuser wie Burgen aussehen.*

PAGES 74 AND 75 *Plettenberg Bay is one of the Garden Route's most fashionable holiday resorts* (LEFT). *Gulls are common residents of Plett's unspoiled Robberg Peninsula* (ABOVE).
PAGES 74 ET 75 *Plettenberg Bay, une des villégiatures des plus prisées de la Garden Route* (À GAUCHE). *Les mouettes sont nombreuses dans la Robberg Peninsula, à Plettenberg Bay* (CI-DESSUS).
SEITE 74 UND 75 *Das wunderschöne Plettenberg Bay ist eines der mondänsten Badeorte an der Garden Route* (LINKS). *Möwen sind verbreitete Bewohner der Robberg-Halbinsel bei Plettenberg Bay* (OBEN) .

PAGES 76 AND 77 *Several nature walks can be taken through pristine Robberg Nature Reserve* (LEFT). *The delicate pansy shell* (BELOW) *is symbolic of Plettenberg Bay, or 'Plett' as it is known. Hobie Beach is the focal point of leisure activities at Plett* (OPPOSITE).

PAGES 76 ET 77 *La Robberg Nature Reserve* (À GAUCHE) *est immaculée et offre un choix de plusieurs itinéraires de promenades. La 'pansy shell' (coquillage-pensée) est symbolique de Plettenberg Bay* (CI-DESSOUS). *Hobie Beach, le centre des activités estivales de Plettenberg Bay* (CI-CONTRE).

SEITE 76 UND 77 *In dem unberührten Robberg Naturschutzgebiet kann man verschiedene Wanderungen unternehmen* (LINKS). *Diese zarte Muschel mit dem Blümchenmuster ist typisch für Plettenberg Bay* (UNTEN). *Hobie Beach – Herzstück der Freizeitgestaltung bei Plettenberg Bay* (GEGENÜBER).

ABOVE AND RIGHT *Built on a rocky promontory overlooking the sea and the lagoon, the luxurious Beacon Island Hotel commands outstanding views and facilities.*

CI-DESSUS ET À DROITE *Le Beacon Island, un hôtel de luxe, est construit sur un promontoire surplombant la mer et le lagon; la vue du sommet est magnifique.*

OBEN UND RECHTS *Auf einer felsigen Landzunge steht das luxuriöse Beacon Island Hotel, mit herrlichen Anlagen und einem wunderbaren Blick über das Meer und die Lagune.*

PAGES 80 AND 81 *Keurbooms River Nature Reserve, a serene retreat in a lagoon and forest setting* (LEFT). *Arch Rock is a well-known landmark at Keurboomstrand* (ABOVE).

PAGES 80 ET 81 *Keurboom River Nature Reserve, entre le lagon et la forêt, est un refuge enchanteur* (À GAUCHE). *'Arch Rock' est bien connu à Keurboomstrand* (CI-DESSUS).

SEITE 80 UND 81 *Keurbooms River Naturschutzgebiet ist ein geruhsamer Erholungsort an der Lagune und wird von Wäldern umgeben* (LINKS). *Der Bogenfels bei Keurboomstrand ist ein landschaftliches Wahrzeichen* (OBEN).

PAGES 82 AND 83 *Nature's Valley beach marks the end of the world-famous Otter Trail.*

PAGES 82 ET 83 *La plage de Nature's Valley, où se termine la piste de l'Otter Trail'.*

SEITE 82 UND 83 *Der Strand bei Nature's Valley ist das Ende des Otter Trail Wanderweges.*

PAGES 84 AND 85 *The Grootrivier Pass* (OPPOSITE) *zigzags through the Tsitsikamma Forest into Nature's Valley in the De Vasselot Nature Reserve. Nature's Valley village is surrounded by forest, home to the vervet monkey* (RIGHT), *and its timber homes* (BELOW) *blend into the woody setting.*

PAGES 84 ET 85 *La Grootrivier Pass* (EN FACE) *se termine à Vasselot Nature Reserve, dans Nature's Valley. Le village est enclavé par la forêt, qui est l'habitat du vervet* (À DROITE). *Ses maisons de bois* (CI-DESSOUS) *se combinent bien avec l'environnement.*

SEITE 84 UND 85 *Diese Seiten Der Grootrivier-Paß* (GEGENÜBER) *windet sich im Zickzack durch den Tsitsikamma-Wald bis nach Nature's Valley im De Vasselot Naturschutzgebiet. Das Dörfchen, Nature's Valley, ist umgeben von Wäldern, wo die Grünmeerkatze* (RECHTS) *beheimatet ist. Die Holzhäuser* (UNTEN) *fügen sich harmonisch in die Waldlandschaft ein.*

LEFT *A picnic site and hiking trail at Kranshoek, close to Plettenberg Bay, offer outstanding views over the rugged cliffs and coastline.*

A GAUCHE *Kranshoek, près de Plettenberg Bay. La vue du sommet, sur le littoral et ses falaises déchiquetées est unique.*

LINKS *Picknickplatz und Wanderweg bei Kranshoek, in der Nähe von Plettenberg Bay, bieten einen einmaligen Blick auf die zerklüfteten Steilhänge und die Küste.*

PAGES 88 AND 89 *Within the Tsitsikamma National Park lies the famed Storms River mouth* (LEFT) *where river and sea meet. Fynbos-covered hills* (ABOVE) *make good viewpoints.*

PAGES 88 ET 89 *La fameuse embouchure de la Storms River* (À GAUCHE), *dans le Tsitsikamma National Park. La vue des collines couvertes de 'fynbos' est magnifique* (CI-DESSUS).

SEITE 88 UND 89 *Die Mündung des Storms River* (LINKS), *wo Fluß und Meer sich begegnen, liegt innerhalb des Tsitsikamma Nationalparks. Von den mit Fynbos bedeckten Hügeln* (OBEN) *hat man eine schöne Aussicht.*

PAGES 90 AND 91 *Timber chalets at the Storms River rest camp overlook the Indian Ocean and provide comfortable accommodation* (ABOVE). *A suspension bridge crosses the Storms River to a viewpoint overlooking the mouth* (RIGHT).

PAGES 90 ET 91 *Les chalets au camp de la Storms River offrent tout le confort* (CI-DESSUS). *Un pont suspendu enjambe la Storms River* (À DROITE). *Il mène à un point de vue surplombant l'embouchure.*

SEITE 90 UND 91 *Holzhäuschen in dem Rastlager bei Storms River bieten komfortable Unterkunft* (OBEN). *Eine Hängebrücke spannt sich über den Storms River bis zu einem Aussichtspunkt, der auf die Mündung hinausblickt* (RECHTS).

PAGES 92 AND 93 *Storms River's rugged beauty is especially magnificent at Skietklip* (OPPOSITE).

PAGES 92 ET 93 *La beauté sauvage de la Storms River se révèle à Skietklip* (CI-CONTRE).

SEITE 92 UND 93 *Die Schönheit des zerklüfteten Storms River ist immer wieder beeindruckend.*

PAGES 94 AND 95 *Storms River, the place of abundant waters* (OPPOSITE). *This waterfall* (RIGHT) *is reached on the first day of the popular Otter Trail.*

PAGES 94 ET 95 *Storms River, où les eaux coulent à flot* (CI-CONTRE). *Cette chute* (À DROITE) *sera atteinte au premier jour sur l'Otter Trail.*

SEITE 94 UND 95 *Storms River: An Wasser herrscht hier kein Mangel. Diesen Wasserfall erreicht man am ersten Tag der Otter Trail Wanderung.*

PAGE 96 *The Paul Sauer Bridge, which was constructed in the 1950s, gives spectacular views of the Storms River Gorge.*

PAGE 96 *Le Paul Sauer Bridge fut bâti dans les années '50. Il offre une vue spectaculaire de la Storms River Gorge.*

SEITE 96 *Die Paul Sauer Brücke, die in den fünfziger Jahren erbaut wurde, bietet einen herrlichen Ausblick über die Flußschlucht des Storms River.*